THE FUTURE OF WRITING WITH GEMINI AI

AN EASY GUIDE FOR EVERYONE

WRITTEN BY EVAN WALTERS

Table of Contents:

Preface: Unleash Your Inner Author with Gemini AI

Do you dream of crafting captivating novels, but feel overwhelmed by blank pages and elusive inspiration? Welcome to the exciting world of writing with AI! This book is your comprehensive guide to using Gemini AI, a cutting-edge artificial intelligence tool designed to empower writers of all levels.

Whether you're a seasoned author seeking to streamline your process or a budding novelist taking your first steps, Gemini AI can be your invaluable companion. Within these pages, you'll discover a treasure trove of strategies to leverage this powerful tool:

- **Ignite your creativity:** Break through writer's block, generate unique story ideas, and develop captivating characters with the help of AI-powered prompts and suggestions.
- **Craft immersive worlds:** Breathe life into your fictional landscapes with evocative descriptions, explore historical details, and

maintain worldbuilding consistency throughout your narrative.

- **Refine your manuscript:** Ensure your writing shines with AI-powered editing assistance. Polish your prose, identify grammatical errors, and enhance readability for a truly captivating experience for your readers.
- **Explore diverse storytelling techniques:** Experiment with different genres, develop natural-sounding dialogue, and craft suspenseful scenes that keep your readers on the edge of their seats.

This book is not a mere instruction manual; it's an invitation to a collaborative writing journey. By understanding Gemini AI's capabilities and limitations, you'll learn to harness its power to fuel your creativity, overcome challenges, and elevate your writing to new heights.

So, grab your cup of coffee, settle in with your favorite writing device, and prepare to embark on an exciting adventure. With Gemini AI as your partner, you have the potential to unlock your inner author and bring your stories to life in a way you never thought possible. Let the writing begin!

Chapter 1: Unveiling Gemini AI: Your Powerful Ally in Book Writing

Welcome to the exciting world of writing with AI! This chapter introduces you to Gemini AI, a cutting-edge artificial intelligence tool designed to empower writers of all levels.

1.1 What is Gemini AI?

Imagine a tireless collaborator who can brainstorm ideas, generate creative text formats, and even help you polish your prose. That's Gemini AI in a nutshell. It's a large language model (think of it as a super-powered AI trained on massive amounts of text data) developed by Google. Gemini AI can understand and respond to your writing needs in a variety of ways:

- **Content Generation:** Stuck staring at a blank page? Gemini AI can help you generate different creative text formats, like descriptions, dialogue prompts, or even character backstories, to jumpstart your writing.
- **Idea Exploration:** Need a spark of inspiration? Gemini AI can help you brainstorm unique story ideas, captivating concepts, and intriguing plot twists to fuel your imagination.
- **Editing and Revision:** Want to ensure your writing is polished and error-free? Gemini AI can assist with identifying grammatical errors and inconsistencies, suggesting

improvements in sentence structure and readability.

1.2 Capabilities of Gemini AI for Writers

Beyond the general functionalities mentioned above, Gemini AI offers a treasure trove of features specifically tailored for writers:

- **Genre-Specific Assistance:** Whether you're crafting a heart-wrenching romance or a thrilling sci-fi adventure, Gemini AI can adapt its assistance to your chosen genre.
- **Character Development:** Need to flesh out your characters? Gemini AI can help you develop rich backstories, complex motivations,

and realistic relationships for your cast.

- **World-Building:** Creating a believable fictional world? Gemini AI can assist with generating evocative descriptions, researching historical details, and maintaining consistency in your worldbuilding elements.
- **Overcoming Writer's Block:** Feeling creatively drained? Gemini AI can provide creative prompts to help you overcome writer's block and reignite your writing flow.

1.3 Benefits of Using Gemini AI for Book Writing

Integrating Gemini AI into your writing process offers a multitude of benefits:

- **Enhanced Creativity:** Break through creative roadblocks and explore new ideas with the help of AI-powered prompts and suggestions.
- **Increased Efficiency:** Streamline your writing process by utilizing AI for tasks like generating content, conducting research, and editing your work.
- **Improved Quality:** Ensure your writing is polished and error-free with AI assistance that identifies grammatical mistakes and suggests improvements in clarity and flow.
- **Boosted Confidence:** Gain valuable support and inspiration from Gemini AI, allowing you to

approach your writing with renewed confidence.

This chapter has provided a foundational understanding of Gemini AI and its potential to transform your book writing journey. In the coming chapters, we'll delve deeper into specific ways to leverage Gemini AI for each stage of the writing process, from brainstorming captivating ideas to polishing your final draft.

Chapter 2: Gearing Up for Success with Gemini AI

Now that you're excited about the possibilities Gemini AI offers, let's dive into setting it up for your book project. This chapter will guide you through navigating the interface, choosing the right Gemini model, and seamlessly integrating it into your writing workflow.

2.1 Understanding the Gemini AI Interface

Imagine Gemini AI as your personal writing assistant with a user-friendly interface. Here's a breakdown of what you can expect:

- **Input Field:** This is where you'll interact with Gemini AI by providing prompts, instructions, or text you want it to analyze.

- **Output Panel:** Here, Gemini AI will display its responses to your prompts, generated content, or suggested edits.
- **Settings Menu:** This menu allows you to customize your experience by selecting the appropriate Gemini model, adjusting output parameters, and exploring other functionalities.

Note: As Gemini AI is still under development, the specific interface elements might change in the future. However, the core functionalities mentioned above will provide a general understanding.

2.2 Choosing the Right Gemini Model for Your Book

Just like having different tools for different jobs, Gemini AI offers various models optimized for specific tasks. Here's how to choose the right one for your book:

- **Genre-Specific Models:** For optimal results, consider using a Gemini model trained on a dataset heavily weighted towards your chosen genre. This ensures the AI understands the nuances of your genre and generates content that aligns with your writing style.
- **Content Focus Models:** Depending on your needs, you might choose a model specializing in content generation, editing and

revision, or even research assistance.

Don't worry, selecting the right model won't be overwhelming! In the future, Gemini AI might offer recommendations based on your project details or writing style.

2.3 Integrating Gemini AI with Your Writing Workflow

The beauty of Gemini AI lies in its seamless integration with your existing writing process. Here are a few ways to incorporate it:

- **Brainstorming Sessions:** Use Gemini AI to generate ideas for plot twists, character development, or even world-building details during your brainstorming sessions.

- **Content Creation:** Stuck on a specific scene or dialogue? Utilize Gemini AI to suggest content variations or provide prompts to get your creative juices flowing again.
- **Editing and Revision:** Run your manuscript through Gemini AI to identify grammatical errors, improve sentence structure, or gain suggestions for enhancing clarity and flow.

Remember, Gemini AI is a powerful tool, but it shouldn't replace your own creative voice. Use it as a collaborator to enhance your writing, not to automate the entire process.

By the end of this chapter, you're equipped with the knowledge to set up Gemini AI and get ready to leverage its power throughout your book writing journey!

Chapter 3: Spark Your Imagination: Brainstorming & Plot Development with Gemini AI

Conjured a captivating concept for your book but hit a wall when it comes to fleshing out the plot? Fear not, writer! This chapter explores how Gemini AI can be your brainstorming partner, igniting your imagination and guiding you through the intricacies of plot development.

3.1 Generating Story Ideas and Concepts

Feeling creatively parched? Let Gemini AI be your muse! Here are some ways to utilize it for story generation:

- **Genre Prompts:** Provide Gemini AI with your chosen genre (fantasy, mystery, romance) and keywords related to your initial ideas. It can then generate unique story concepts that spark your interest.
- **Character-Driven Inspiration:** Do you have a compelling character in mind? Describe them to Gemini AI and request story ideas that explore their motivations, conflicts, and potential journeys.
- **"What If" Scenarios:** Pose intriguing "what if" questions to

Gemini AI. For example, "What if humanity discovered a portal to another dimension?" and see where its creative responses take you.

Remember: Don't be afraid to experiment with different prompts and refine them based on the generated ideas.

3.2 Developing Character Arcs and Relationships

Compelling characters are the backbone of any story. Here's how Gemini AI can assist in crafting them:

- **Character Backstory Prompts:** Provide basic details about your characters, and utilize Gemini AI to generate rich backstories that flesh out their personalities, motivations, and potential flaws.

- **Relationship Exploration:** Describe two characters and their initial dynamic. Gemini AI can suggest potential conflicts, turning points, and how their relationship might evolve throughout the story.
- **Character Voice Development:** Struggling to solidify a character's voice? Write a short passage from their perspective and have Gemini AI analyze it, suggesting improvements that capture their unique personality.

Pro Tip: Use Gemini AI's generated content as a springboard for further development. You can always add your own creative twists and refine the ideas to fit your vision.

3.3 Creating Plot Outlines and Storyboards

Once you have a grasp of your characters and core ideas, let's move on to structuring your plot. Here's where Gemini AI can be your organizational partner:

- **Plot Point Brainstorming:** List down the major events you envision in your story. Gemini AI can help generate additional plot points, suggest consequences of character actions, and ensure a logical narrative flow.
- **Scene Outlining:** Provide a brief description of a scene and have Gemini AI create a more detailed outline, including potential dialogue prompts, character

interactions, and setting descriptions.

- **Storyboard Creation:** With key plot points identified, use Gemini AI to generate visual snippets or textual summaries for each scene, essentially creating a storyboard to visualize your narrative flow.

Remember, plot outlines and storyboards are flexible tools. Don't be afraid to adapt them as your story evolves and new ideas emerge.

By incorporating these strategies, Gemini AI can become your brainstorming companion, helping you transform initial sparks into a well-developed plot that will keep your readers engaged. The next chapter will delve into how Gemini AI can further empower you in world-building and research for your book.

Chapter 4: Building Worlds & Research Made Easy with Gemini AI

Have you envisioned a fantastical world or a meticulously detailed historical setting for your book? This chapter explores how Gemini AI can be your world-building companion and research assistant, ensuring your fictional landscapes are both captivating and believable.

4.1 Building Fictional Worlds with Descriptive Prompts

Crafting a captivating fictional world requires vivid descriptions that transport readers to your imagination. Here's how Gemini AI can assist:

- **Sensory Details:** Describe the general atmosphere of a location (e.g., a bustling marketplace) and have Gemini AI generate details that appeal to the five senses (sight, sound, smell, taste, touch). This creates a more immersive experience for your readers.
- **Cultural Nuances:** Provide Gemini AI with the basic structure of a fictional society. It can then generate details about their customs, traditions, and even clothing styles, enriching your world-building.
- **Geographical Features:** Describe the broad landscape of your world (e.g., a vast desert) and have

Gemini AI create details about specific geographical features like unique flora and fauna, or natural wonders.

Remember: The key is to provide clear and detailed prompts to elicit the most relevant and evocative responses from Gemini AI.

4.2 Researching Historical Events and Cultural Details

Whether you're writing a historical fiction novel or incorporating real-world elements into your fantasy world, accuracy is crucial. Here's how Gemini AI can be your research assistant:

- **Fact-Checking and Verification:** Unsure about a historical detail or cultural practice? Utilize Gemini AI to verify information you've found elsewhere, ensuring your portrayal remains consistent with historical records.

- **In-Depth Exploration:** Provide a starting point (e.g., the Renaissance period) and have Gemini AI generate relevant details about social structures, political climate, or everyday life during that time.
- **Terminology and Vocabulary:** Struggling to find the appropriate terminology for a specific historical period or cultural context? Gemini AI can suggest relevant terms and phrases, enhancing the authenticity of your writing.

Important Note: While Gemini AI is a powerful tool, it's not a substitute for in-depth historical research. Always consult credible sources alongside using AI assistance.

4.3 Maintaining Worldbuilding Cohesion Throughout the Book

As your story unfolds, ensure the elements of your world-building remain consistent. Here's how Gemini AI can help:

- **Maintaining Internal Consistency:** As you write, use Gemini AI to double-check details about your world. This helps you avoid inconsistencies that might confuse readers.
- **Cross-referencing Information:** Create a central document outlining key aspects of your world-building. Gemini AI can then analyze your manuscript and flag

any potential inconsistencies between your writing and the established details.

- **Tracking Details:** Feeling overwhelmed with the intricate details of your world? Utilize Gemini AI to help you organize and track information about your fictional landscape, ensuring a cohesive experience for your readers.

By leveraging these strategies, Gemini AI can become an invaluable tool for crafting immersive and believable worlds that serve as the backdrop for your captivating story. The next chapter will explore how Gemini AI can help you overcome writer's block and generate compelling content to bring your narrative to life.

Chapter 5: Conquering Writer's Block & Content Generation with Gemini AI

Every writer faces the dreaded writer's block. But fear not! This chapter equips you with strategies to overcome creative roadblocks and leverage Gemini AI's content generation capabilities to fuel your writing journey.

5.1 Breaking Through the Block

Staring at a blank page can be paralyzing. Here's how Gemini AI can reignite your creative spark:

- **"What If" Prompts:** Pose intriguing "what if" scenarios related to your story's existing plot points. Gemini AI's response can introduce unexpected twists or consequences, jolting you out of a creative rut.

- **Character-Driven Prompts:** Describe a character facing a dilemma and have Gemini AI generate their internal monologue, potential actions, or unexpected reactions. This can breathe fresh life into your scenes.
- **Setting Prompts:** Provide a brief description of your story's setting and have Gemini AI generate unexpected details, hidden dangers, or intriguing encounters that could occur within that location.

Remember: Don't be afraid to experiment with different prompts and refine them based on the results. Sometimes, even seemingly irrelevant responses from Gemini AI can spark a new idea.

5.2 Expanding Your Horizons: Scene and Dialogue Development

Once you have a spark of inspiration, here's how Gemini AI can help you develop it into compelling content:

- **Scene Expansion:** Provide a basic outline of a scene and have Gemini AI generate details about the setting, character interactions, or potential conflicts. This can help you flesh out a scene from a skeletal outline to a vibrant narrative segment.
- **Dialogue Prompts:** Describe the context of a conversation and have Gemini AI generate natural-sounding dialogue for your

characters. You can even specify the desired tone (serious, humorous, etc.) for further customization.

- **Description Enhancement:** Provide a basic description of a location or character and have Gemini AI enrich it with sensory details and evocative language, bringing your scene or character to life for the reader.

Pro Tip: Don't rely solely on AI-generated content. Use it as a springboard for your own creativity, adding your unique voice and style to the suggestions provided.

5.3 Exploring Style & Perspective

Experimenting with different writing styles and character perspectives can add depth and intrigue to your narrative. Here's how Gemini AI can assist:

- **Genre Exploration:** Provide a scene or dialogue snippet written in your usual style and have Gemini AI rewrite it in the style of a different genre (e.g., from romance to sci-fi). This can help you explore alternative approaches and potentially unlock new creative directions for your story.

- **Character Perspective Shifts:** Write a scene from one character's perspective and have Gemini AI rewrite it from another character's viewpoint. This can reveal hidden motives, introduce unexpected twists, and provide a more well-rounded narrative.

- **Narrative Voice Variations:** Provide a passage written in your usual narrative voice and have Gemini AI suggest alternative phrasings or sentence structures, helping you explore different storytelling styles that might resonate better with your readers.

By incorporating these strategies, Gemini AI can become your creative partner, helping you overcome writer's block, generate compelling content, and explore diverse narrative approaches to bring your story to life. The next chapter will delve into how Gemini AI can assist you in refining your manuscript through the editing and revision process.

Chapter 6: Refining Your Manuscript: Editing & Revision with Gemini AI

Crafting a captivating story is only half the battle. Now comes the crucial stage of editing and revision. This chapter explores how Gemini AI can be your eagle-eyed companion, assisting you in polishing your manuscript and ensuring it shines for your readers.

6.1 Grammar & Consistency Check

Even the most seasoned writers can make grammatical errors or stylistic inconsistencies. Here's how Gemini AI can be your proofreading partner:

- **Grammar and Mechanics:** Run your manuscript through Gemini AI to identify grammatical errors, typos, and punctuation mistakes. This helps ensure your writing is polished and error-free.

- **Consistency Analysis:** Provide Gemini AI with details about your established writing style (e.g., tense, point of view) and have it analyze your manuscript for inconsistencies. This helps maintain a smooth reading experience.

- **Word Choice Optimization:** Unsure about a particular word choice? Gemini AI can suggest synonyms or alternative phrasings that might better convey your intended meaning or enhance the overall flow of your writing.

Remember: Don't blindly accept all suggestions. Use your own judgment to determine if the proposed edits improve your writing or maintain your desired voice.

6.2 Readability & Pacing Enhancements

A well-written story should be a smooth and engaging read. Here's how Gemini AI can help you elevate your manuscript's readability and pacing:

- **Sentence Structure Analysis:** Gemini AI can analyze your sentence structure and suggest improvements for clarity, conciseness, or variety. This ensures your writing is easy to understand and avoids monotonous sentence patterns.

- **Pacing Checks:** Feeling like your story drags in certain sections? Utilize Gemini AI to identify areas with potentially slow pacing and suggest ways to add tension, suspense, or action to keep your readers engaged.
- **Readability Score Analysis:** Gemini AI might be able to provide readability scores, which estimate the reading difficulty level of your text. Use this as a guide to ensure your writing is accessible to your target audience.

Important Note: Readability scores are just one metric. Ultimately, trust your own judgment and writing style when making revisions.

6.3 Beyond Mechanics: Exploring Character & Plot Cohesion

Editing goes beyond grammar and mechanics. Here's how Gemini AI can assist in ensuring your story's narrative elements are cohesive:

- **Character Consistency Checks:** Run your manuscript through Gemini AI and have it analyze character actions and dialogue for consistency with their established personalities and motivations. This helps avoid character inconsistencies that might confuse readers.
- **Plot Hole Identification:** Describe key plot points and have Gemini AI analyze them for logical flow and potential inconsistencies. This can help you identify plot holes or

areas where cause-and-effect relationships need strengthening.

- **Emotional Arc Evaluation:** Describe the intended emotional journey of your characters and have Gemini AI analyze your writing to see if it effectively conveys those emotions to the reader. This ensures your story resonates with your audience on an emotional level.

Pro Tip: Don't rely solely on AI for editing. Utilize beta readers, critique partners, or professional editing services for a comprehensive revision process.

By incorporating these strategies, Gemini AI can become your invaluable editing companion, helping you identify errors, refine your writing style, and ensure your manuscript is polished, clear, and engaging for your readers. The next chapter delves into how Gemini AI can further enhance your character development and dialogue writing.

Chapter 7: Character Craft & Captivating Dialogue: Unleashing Potential with Gemini AI

Compelling characters and natural-sounding dialogue are the lifeblood of any story. This chapter explores how Gemini AI can be your character development coach and dialogue doctor, helping you craft characters that resonate and conversations that flow.

7.1 Fleshing Out Character Backstories and Motivations

Well-developed characters with rich backstories and complex motivations drive reader engagement. Here's how

Gemini AI can be your character development partner:

- **Backstory Prompts:** Provide basic details about your characters (appearance, personality traits) and have Gemini AI generate detailed backstories that explore their formative experiences, defining moments, and hidden desires.
- **Motivation Analysis:** Describe a character's actions and have Gemini AI analyze their underlying motivations, potential fears, or hidden agendas. This helps you create multi-dimensional characters with believable actions.
- **Character Relationship Exploration:** Describe the dynamic between two characters

and have Gemini AI generate potential conflicts, turning points, and how their relationship might evolve throughout the story.

Remember: Use AI-generated backstories and motivations as a springboard for further development. Refine these suggestions to ensure they align with your overall vision for your characters.

7.2 Generating Natural-Sounding Dialogue and Banter

Dialogue breathes life into your characters and drives the plot forward. Here's how Gemini AI can be your dialogue doctor:

- **Character-Specific Dialogue Prompts:** Describe a situation and a character involved. Gemini AI can generate dialogue tailored to that specific character's voice, personality, and emotional state.

- **Dialogue Expansion:** Provide a snippet of conversation and have Gemini AI expand it with natural-sounding follow-up lines, witty banter, or emotional outbursts, depending on the context.

- **Subtext and Emotional Nuances:** Describe a conversation and have Gemini AI suggest ways to incorporate subtext, hidden meanings, or unspoken emotions within the dialogue, making it more nuanced and engaging.

Pro Tip: Don't replace your own creativity entirely. Use AI-generated dialogue as a starting point, refining it to ensure it reflects your unique writing style and character voices.

7.3 Creating Distinct Voices for Multiple Characters

A cast of characters with distinct voices is crucial to avoiding confusion and making your story memorable. Here's how Gemini AI can assist:

- **Voice Analysis:** Provide samples of dialogue written in different character voices and have Gemini AI analyze them, suggesting improvements for maintaining consistency and distinctiveness.
- **Dialogue Style Exploration:** Describe a scene and have Gemini AI generate dialogue options in different styles (formal, informal, humorous) to help you

determine the most appropriate voice for each character in that specific context.

- **Character Dialect Exploration:** If your story involves characters with regional dialects, utilize Gemini AI to research and suggest appropriate vocabulary or phrasings, ensuring authenticity in their dialogue.

Remember: While AI can be a helpful tool, it's still under development. Double-check any dialect suggestions from Gemini AI with credible sources to ensure accuracy.

By incorporating these strategies, Gemini AI can become your partner in crafting captivating characters with depth and nuance, and generating natural-sounding dialogue that brings your characters to life and propels your story forward. The next chapter will explore how Gemini AI can elevate your world descriptions and sensory details, further immersing your readers in the world you've created.

Chapter 8: Immersive Descriptions & Sensory Details: Painting Your World with Gemini AI

In captivating storytelling, vivid descriptions transport readers directly into your fictional world. This chapter explores how Gemini AI can be your descriptive collaborator, helping you craft immersive settings with rich sensory details that bring your story to life.

8.1 Crafting Immersive Descriptions of Settings

Memorable settings leave a lasting impression on readers. Here's how Gemini AI can be your descriptive partner:

- **Sensory Prompts:** Describe a location in general terms (e.g., a bustling marketplace) and have Gemini AI generate details that appeal to all five senses (sight, sound, smell, taste, touch). This creates a more immersive experience for your readers.
- **Atmosphere Enhancement:** Describe the overall mood or atmosphere of a setting (e.g., eerie forest) and have Gemini AI suggest specific details that evoke that atmosphere, like creaking branches or damp earth underfoot.
- **Show, Don't Tell:** Provide a basic description of a location and have Gemini AI rewrite it using more evocative language and sensory

details, allowing readers to "see" the setting in their minds.

Remember: Effective descriptions are concise yet impactful. Use AI-generated details to enhance your existing descriptions, avoiding information overload for your readers.

8.2 Enhancing Scenes with Sensory Details

Sensory details bring your scenes to life and allow readers to connect with your story on a deeper emotional level. Here's how Gemini AI can assist:

- **Sight Details:** Describe a scene visually (e.g., a vast mountain range) and have Gemini AI generate specific details about colors, textures, or unique features that make the scene visually captivating.

- **Sound Details:** Describe a scene's ambient soundscape (e.g., a quiet library) and have Gemini AI suggest additional sounds that enhance the atmosphere, like the rustling of pages or the distant hum of conversation.

- **Smell and Taste Details:** When appropriate for your story's genre, utilize Gemini AI to suggest evocative smells and tastes that further immerse readers in the scene (e.g., the aroma of freshly baked bread in a bakery).

Pro Tip: Don't overwhelm readers with excessive sensory details. Use them strategically to highlight important aspects of your scene and evoke specific emotions.

8.3 Maintaining Worldbuilding Cohesion Throughout the Book

As your story unfolds, ensure the elements of your world-building remain consistent. Here's how Gemini AI can be your worldbuilding companion:

- **Sensory Detail Consistency Checks:** Run your manuscript through Gemini AI and have it analyze your use of sensory details across different scenes. This helps ensure a cohesive sensory experience for your readers, avoiding inconsistencies in how you describe your world.
- **Internal Logic Analysis:** Describe a specific aspect of your world

(e.g., the magic system) and have Gemini AI analyze your writing to identify potential inconsistencies or areas where the internal logic of your world might need clarification.

- **Sensory Detail Cross-Referencing:** Create a central document outlining key sensory details associated with different locations or elements in your world. Gemini AI can then analyze your manuscript and flag any inconsistencies between your writing and the established details.

By incorporating these strategies, Gemini AI can become your partner in crafting immersive and sensory-rich descriptions. This will allow you to create a captivating world that your readers can truly step into and experience alongside your characters. The next chapter delves into advanced techniques for experienced writers, exploring how Gemini AI can further enhance your storytelling journey.

Chapter 9: Power Up Your Storytelling: Advanced Techniques with Gemini AI

Congratulations! You've mastered the fundamentals of utilizing Gemini AI to elevate your writing process. This chapter delves into advanced techniques specifically tailored for experienced writers, allowing you to push the boundaries of your creativity and explore new storytelling avenues with the help of AI.

9.1 Genre Exploration and Experimentation

Ever dreamt of writing outside your comfort zone? Here's how Gemini AI can be your genre-bending partner:

- **Genre-Specific Prompts:** Provide a basic story concept and specify a genre you've never written in before. Gemini AI can generate creative prompts and narrative elements tailored to that specific genre, helping you explore unfamiliar territory.
- **Style Mimicry:** Provide a passage written by a renowned author in a particular genre and have Gemini AI analyze their writing style. It can then suggest ways to incorporate elements of that style into your own writing, allowing you to experiment with different narrative voices.
- **Genre Mashup Exploration:** Feeling adventurous? Describe two contrasting genres (e.g., sci-fi

romance) and have Gemini AI brainstorm potential storylines or character concepts that blend these seemingly disparate genres, creating a unique and innovative narrative.

Remember: Experimentation is key! Don't be afraid to step outside your comfort zone and explore new storytelling possibilities with the help of AI-generated prompts and suggestions.

9.2 Subplot Development and Foreshadowing

Intricate subplots and well-placed foreshadowing can elevate your story's complexity and keep readers engaged. Here's how Gemini AI can assist:

- **Character-Driven Subplots:** Describe one of your main characters and have Gemini AI generate a potential subplot that revolves around them, adding depth and intrigue to their narrative arc.
- **Thematic Subplots:** Describe a central theme in your story and have Gemini AI brainstorm a subplot that reinforces or explores that theme from a different angle, enriching your narrative.
- **Foreshadowing Prompts:** Describe a future event you want to foreshadow and have Gemini AI suggest subtle hints or clues you can integrate into your earlier chapters, building anticipation and rewarding attentive readers.

Pro Tip: Don't reveal too much too soon! Use AI-generated foreshadowing elements strategically to create a sense of mystery and keep readers guessing.

9.3 Crafting Suspense and Cliffhangers

A well-placed cliffhanger can leave readers desperate to turn the page. Here's how Gemini AI can be your suspense-building partner:

- **"What If" Scenarios for Stakes:** Describe a pivotal scene and have Gemini AI generate potential consequences or "what if" scenarios that raise the stakes and heighten the tension for your characters.
- **Character Conflict Prompts:** Describe a scene of conflict

between two characters and have Gemini AI suggest ways to escalate the tension, introduce unexpected twists, or leave the outcome hanging, creating a captivating cliffhanger.

- **Suspenseful Description Prompts:** Provide a basic description of a setting and have Gemini AI generate details that build suspense and a sense of impending danger, drawing your readers deeper into the narrative.

Remember: Effective suspense hinges on a well-established narrative foundation. Use AI-generated prompts to enhance existing scenes, not to replace the core elements of your plot.

By incorporating these advanced techniques, you can leverage Gemini

AI to push the boundaries of your storytelling, experiment with new genres and narrative styles, and craft captivating stories that keep your readers on the edge of their seats. The final chapter will explore the evolving landscape of AI-powered writing tools and the ethical considerations surrounding their use.

Chapter 10: The Future of Book Writing with AI: A Collaborative Journey

We've explored how Gemini AI can become your writing companion, but the story doesn't end here. This chapter delves into the ever-evolving landscape of AI-powered writing tools and the ethical considerations that accompany this exciting new frontier in storytelling.

10.1 AI as a Co-Creator, Not a Replacement

AI writing assistants like Gemini AI are here to empower writers, not replace them. They can brainstorm ideas, generate content, and identify areas for improvement, but the heart and soul of storytelling remains firmly in the hands of the human writer.

10.2 The Ethical Landscape of AI-Assisted Writing

As AI writing tools become more sophisticated, ethical considerations arise. Here are some key points to remember:

- **Originality and Authorship:** Always strive to maintain your own creative voice and style, even when utilizing AI-generated content. Strive to ensure your work is original and reflects your unique vision.
- **Transparency and Disclosure:** Be transparent about your use of AI writing tools. If applicable, consider mentioning AI assistance

in your acknowledgements or author's note.

- **Accuracy and Bias Detection:** Be mindful of potential biases that might exist within AI algorithms. Fact-check all AI-generated information and ensure your writing accurately reflects your intended message.

10.3 The Future of AI and Storytelling

The future of AI-powered writing tools is brimming with possibilities. Here's a glimpse into what's on the horizon:

- **Enhanced Genre-Specific Techniques:** Expect AI to become even more adept at specific genres, providing tailored suggestions and content creation aligned with the unique conventions of different writing styles.

- **Advanced Research and Fact-Checking:** AI might evolve to become even more comprehensive research assistants, providing writers with accurate and relevant information seamlessly integrated into the writing workflow.

- **Personalized Storytelling Experiences:** Imagine AI tools that can tailor narratives based on reader preferences, creating interactive or choose-your-own-adventure stories.

The future of book writing with AI is a collaborative one. As AI capabilities continue to develop, writers will have access to ever-more powerful tools to craft captivating stories, explore uncharted creative territories, and engage readers in innovative ways.

By understanding the potential and limitations of AI writing assistants, and approaching them with a critical and creative mindset, you can ensure they elevate your writing journey and empower you to tell the stories that ignite your imagination.

www.ingramcontent.com/pod-product-compliance
Lightning Source LLC
LaVergne TN
LVHW051741050326
832903LV00023B/1043